St. Rose of Lima

Exploring Science

The Exploring Science series is designed to meet all the Attainment Targets in the National Science Curriculum for levels 3 to 6. The topics in each book are divided into knowledge and understanding sections, followed by exploration. Carefully planned Test Yourself questions at the end of each topic ensure that the student has mastered the appropriate level of attainment specified in the Curriculum.

EXPLORING
EARTH IN SPACE

Robert Stephenson and Roger Browne

Illustrated by Jenny Hughes

Exploring Science

Earth in Space
Electricity
Energy Sources
Forces and Structures
Light
Magnets
Ourselves
Plants
Soil and Rocks
Sound
Uses of Energy
Weather

Cover illustrations:
Left The Earth, as viewed from the surface of the Moon.
Right above An astronomer using the 20-inch Carnegie Double Astrographic Telescope in the USA.
Right below A diagram of our solar system.

Frontispiece Sunspots can be seen clearly on the lower part of the Sun. These spots will 'move' as the Sun rotates.

Editor: Elizabeth Spiers
Designer: Marilyn Clay
Series designer: Ross George

First published in 1991 by
Wayland (Publishers) Ltd
61 Western Road, Hove
East Sussex BN3 1JD, England

© Copyright 1991 Wayland (Publishers) Ltd

British Library Cataloguing in Publication Data
Stephenson, Robert 1950–
  Earth in space.
  1. Earth sciences
  I. Title. II. Browne, Roger
  550

  ISBN 0-7502-0084-7

Typeset by Direct Image Photosetting Ltd, Hove, Sussex, England
Printed in Italy by G. Canale & C.S.p.A., Turin
Bound in France by A.G.M.

Contents

The Blue Planet	6
Old ideas	8
The seasons	10
The Sun's position	14
Telling time by the Sun	16
Time zones	20
Sun and Earth	24
The Moon – our satellite	26
The Moon's surface	28
Eclipses	30
The solar system	32
The planets	34
The Sun – our star	36
The galaxy – our star city	38
Constellations	40
Navigation by the Sun	42
Spaceship Earth	44
Glossary	46
Books to read	47
Index	48

THE BLUE PLANET

No matter which country we come from, which language we speak, whether we live in a town or in the country, near the sea or in the mountains, we all live on the surface of the same slowly spinning planet called the Earth. It is sometimes called the 'Blue Planet', because two-thirds of its surface is covered in water.

The Earth is a giant ball nearly 13,000 km across and 40,000 km all the way around its widest part. We live on the thinnest outer layer, where all life is sustained by air, water and sunlight. All life exists in this thin layer, just 13 km deep on the surface of the Earth. Imagine that the Earth is a model 1 m across; this life-supporting layer would be just 1 mm thick. Some creatures live in the depths of the ocean – about 3 km below sea level. At about 10 km above sea level there is not enough air for living things to breathe.

The Earth is sometimes known as the 'Blue Planet', because two-thirds of its surface is covered in water.

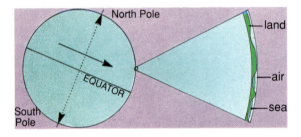

A diagram to show the direction of rotation of the Earth.

Our planet does not just hang motionless in space. It has two important kinds of movement. It spins one complete turn every 24 hours. Seen from above the North Pole, the spin is anti-clockwise. We can tell that the Earth spins, because the Sun 'rises' every morning and 'sets' every night. During the day, your side of the Earth is facing the Sun, and at night, your side is turned away from the Sun.

The Earth also travels around the Sun, in a nearly circular orbit (path) that takes just over 365 days to complete. The length of the orbit is 940 million km. The Earth travels 2.5 million km every day along its orbit, at a speed of 30 km every second. We do not notice this speed because we are on the planet's surface, and there is nothing very close in space to look at as we rush past.

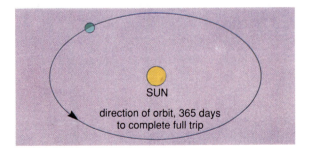

A diagram to show the Earth's orbit around the Sun (not to scale).

ACTIVITY

> **YOU NEED**
>
> - **a magnetic compass**

1. Study the picture showing the Earth's spin. Notice which way is east and which is west.
2. From which compass direction would you expect to see the Sun appear in the morning? In which compass direction would it disappear at night? Check your answers using the compass.

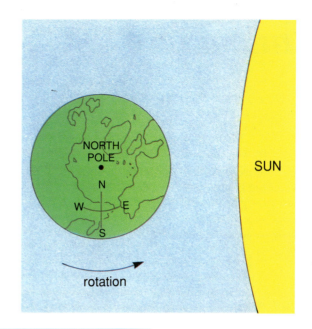

MODELLING THE EARTH'S SPIN

> **YOU NEED**
>
> - **a flashlight**
> - **a dark room**
> - **a friend**

1. Stand in a dark room and ask a friend to shine a flashlight on to your head. This represents the Sun.
2. Face away from it.
3. Imagine your head is the Earth. Turn anti-clockwise (to your left) slowly until you see the flashlight. Keep turning until it disappears.

4. What happened to the 'Sun' as you turned?

TEST YOURSELF

1. How thick is the air and water layer on the surface of the Earth that contains all life?
2. What are the two most important kinds of movement of the Earth?
3. How can we tell that the Earth is spinning?

OLD IDEAS

You know that we live on a giant spinning ball called the Earth, which orbits around the Sun once a year. This was not always common knowledge. The people of ancient India thought the Earth was a flat disc, held up by four elephants standing on the back of a huge turtle.

Over 23,000 years ago, the Greek philosopher Aristotle discovered that the world is a round ball. He looked at the Pole Star, which is always seen in the same part of the sky. When he saw it from Greece, it was 40° above the horizon, but when he saw it from Egypt, it was at a height of only 30°. He knew this meant we lived on a spherical (ball-like) planet. The diagram will help you understand.

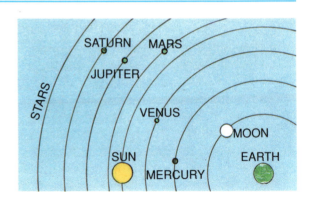

A diagram to show how Aristotle viewed the Earth's position in space.

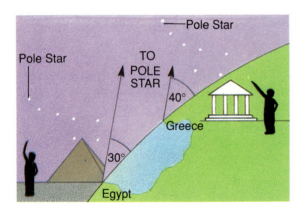

A diagram to show how Aristotle discovered that the Earth is spherical.

Although the ancient astronomers knew the Earth was like a ball in space, they were wrong about its position. They believed that the Sun, Moon, planets (they had found five of them) and stars moved round the Earth, which was at the centre of everything. It is easy to see how they made this mistake. If you do not know that the Earth is spinning, the only way to explain the constant 'movement' of the Sun, Moon, planets and stars is to imagine that they move around the Earth. It was not until 1543 that the Pole, Copernicus, published his idea that the Sun was in the centre, with the Earth and planets moving round it.

The seventeenth-century Italian scientist, Galileo, agreed with Copernicus' view that the Sun was at the centre of the Universe.

ACTIVITIES

1 There were many other important astronomers at the time of Aristotle and Copernicus. Find out about Ptolemy and why he was so important to our understanding of ancient Greek astronomy. Find out about the discoveries of the Italian scientist, Galileo, and his troubles with the Church. What did Galileo make which helped him with his observations?

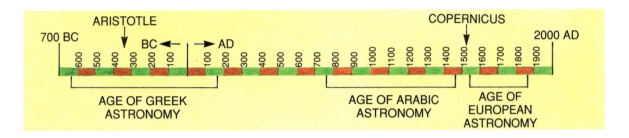

2 Copy the timeline above. Add Galileo and Ptolemy. You will add more to it as you read this book.

3 How do the four drawings of the ship steaming towards you help to explain that we live on a spherical planet? Use the information on page 8 to help you with your answer.

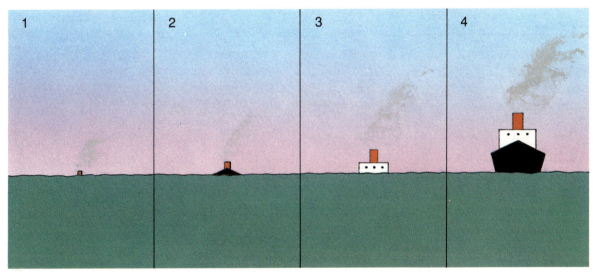

TEST YOURSELF

1. Who discovered that the Earth is spherical?
2. Why did ancient astronomers mistakenly believe that the Earth was circled by the Sun, Moon and planets?

THE SEASONS

You know that the slow spin of the Earth gives us day and night. Each evening, the rotating Earth carries you out of the light of the Sun. At night, you are in the Earth's shadow. The Sun rises again as the Earth turns us back into the Sun's light.

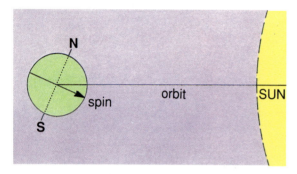

Part of the Earth's orbit, to show the tilt of the Earth.

If the spinning Earth was upright compared with its orbit round the Sun, each day would be 12 hours and each night would be 12 hours, all over the Earth. We know this is not true – days are shorter in the winter and longer in the summer. This is because the Earth is not upright in its orbit: it leans over at 23.5° from the vertical.

As the Earth travels round the Sun, the poles keep pointing at the same places in space. At one point in the Earth's orbit, the North Pole leans towards the Sun and the South Pole leans away from the Sun and is in the Earth's shadow. This is the northern midsummer and southern midwinter. At this time, the North Pole has 24 hours of daylight and there are 24 hours of darkness at the South Pole. Sydney, Australia, has only 8.5 hours of daylight each day and New York, USA, has 16.5 hours. Six months later, it is the South Pole that tilts towards the Sun; this is the southern midsummer and northern midwinter. Between summer and winter, the day length gradually changes as the Earth

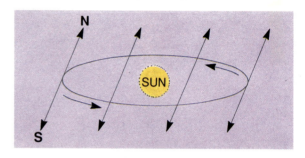

A diagram showing how, as the Earth travels around its orbit, the poles always point to the same place in space.

moves around its orbit. This changing day length creates the seasons. A long day brings more warmth and light than a day with very few hours. This is why summer and spring are seasons of growth, and winter and autumn are not.

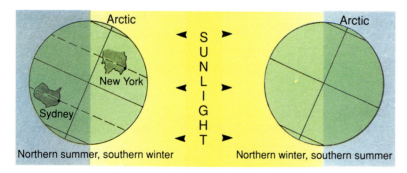

A diagram to show the positions of the Earth in the northern midsummer and northern midwinter, in relation to the Sun.

A country landscape in late spring (above) and in winter (below). These seasonal changes are caused by the tilt of the Earth.

ACTIVITY

A MODEL TO SHOW THE SEASONS

You have seen that the tilt of the Earth gives us seasons and creates the changing number of daylight hours that go with them. A model of the Earth and Sun will help you understand how this happens.

YOU NEED

- a rubber ball with a clear halfway line (this is the equator)
- a drawing pin
- Blutak
- a small block of wood
- a spotlight
- a large sheet of paper
- felt-tip pens
- a protractor
- cardboard
- scissors
- an atlas

1. Use the protractor and scissors to cut a wedge of cardboard with an angle of 23.5°.

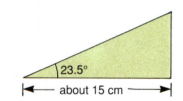

2. Fix the drawing pin to the wood block with Blutak.

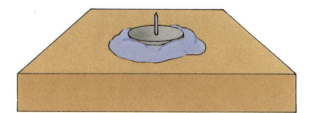

3. Find your latitude in the atlas. This is your distance from the equator, measured as an angle.
4. Use a felt pen to mark your latitude on the ball. Turn the ball against a finger on the pole so that the pen draws the latitude parallel to the ball's equator line.

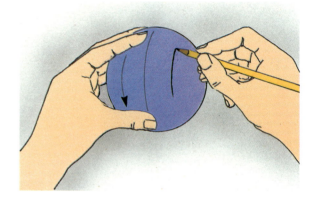

5. Push the ball on to the drawing pin so that the equator seam is in line with the 23.5° cardboard cut-out.

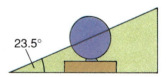

6. Draw a large circle on the paper and mark the centre. This circle is the orbit.

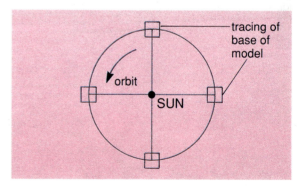

7. Trace around the base of the model Earth, as shown, so that you can move the Earth around the orbit and keep the tilt of the Earth in the same direction.
8. Place your model in the midsummer (northern) position. Shine the lamp on to the Earth across the centre of the orbit.

9. Trace around the line where day and night meet. Notice how much of your latitude line is in daylight.
10. Move the Earth to each of the four places and draw on the night/day boundary line.

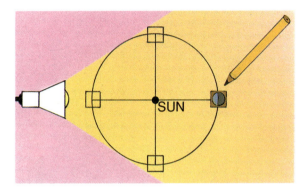

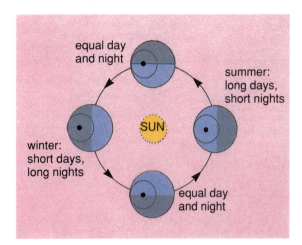

PLOTTING THE HOURS OF DAYLIGHT

1. Use the table of sunrise and sunset to work out the hours of daylight in the middle of each month.
2. Draw a graph of daylight hours against date.
3. Find two months with 12 hours of day and 12 hours of night.
4. Find the month with the longest daylight hours and the one with the shortest.

Time of sunrise and sunset at 50°N		
DATE	SUNRISE (GMT)	SUNSET (GMT)
mid-January	8.00 am	4.03 pm
mid-February	7.15 am	5.15 pm
mid-March	6.00 am	6.00 pm
mid-April	5.00 am	7.00 pm
mid-May	4.15 am	7.45 pm
mid-June	3.45 am	8.15 pm
mid-July	4.00 am	8.15 pm
mid-August	4.45 am	7.30 pm
mid-September	5.30 am	6.25 pm
mid-October	6.15 am	5.15 pm
mid-November	7.15 am	4.15 pm
mid-December	8.00 am	4.00 pm

TEST YOURSELF

1. Why are there not 12 hours of daylight and 12 hours of night all year round?
2. What are the positions of the North and South Poles during southern midwinter?
3. Which are the two months that have 12 hours of day and 12 hours of night?

THE SUN'S POSITION

You have seen that the number of daylight hours changes as the Earth orbits the Sun (see page 8). This is caused by the tilt of the Earth, which also changes the Sun's position in the sky during the year. The first of these changes is shown in the diagram opposite.

Diagram A shows midday on 21 June, which is midsummer in the northern hemisphere (the part of the Earth that is north of the equator). The observer is at 52° north of the equator (latitude 52°N) and sees the Sun at an angle of 61.5° to the horizon. Diagram B shows midday on 21 December (midwinter in the northern hemisphere). Here, the observer at 52°N sees the Sun at an angle of only 14.5°. So the Sun rises higher in the sky in summer than it does in winter. You can see the effect of this if you look at your shadow on sunny days throughout the year. It will be much longer at 15.00 on a winter's day than at 15.00 on a summer's day.

The other important change in the Sun's position during the year is where it rises and sets. You know (see page 6) that the Sun rises in the east and sets in the west as the Earth turns. This is generally true. However, in

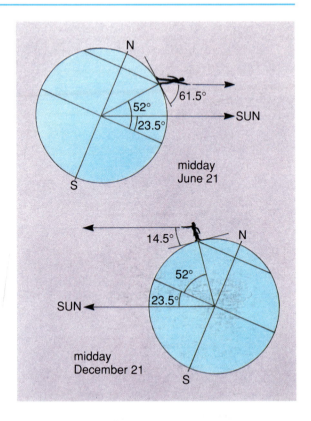

summer, the Sun rises and sets further north. In winter, it rises and sets further south. The diagram below will help you to understand why this happens.

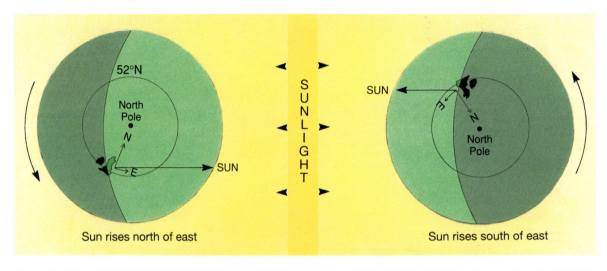

ACTIVITY

THE POSITION OF SUNSET

YOU NEED

- a magnetic compass
- a paper and pencil
- sunny evenings

1 Go outside at home and draw the skyline all around you.

2 Use the compass to label your panorama with north, south, east and west.

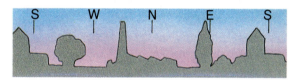

3 Mark the position of sunset on your panorama. Label it with the date. Keep adding this information once a month for several months. What do you notice?

CHANGING ANGLE OF THE MIDDAY SUN

YOU NEED

- an open, level place
- a stick about 110 cm long
- a protractor
- a ruler
- paper and pencil

1 Push the stick into the ground so that 1 m remains above the ground. Use the protractor to check that the stick is vertical.

2 Once a week at noon, Greenwich Mean Time, measure the length of the shadow.

3 Use the table to find the angle of the Sun above the horizon.

LENGTH OF SHADOW (CM)									
373	275	214	173	143	119	100	84	70	58
15°	20°	25°	30°	35°	40°	45°	50°	55°	60°
ANGLE OF SUN ABOVE HORIZON									

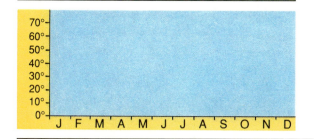

4 Keep a record of the dates and angles to draw a graph. What do you notice?

TEST YOURSELF

1. At what time of the year does the Sun rise:
- in the south-east?
- in the north-east?

2. How does the angle of the Sun in the sky change during the year?

TELLING TIME BY THE SUN

You have seen that the Sun appears at dawn further north in the northern summer and further south in the northern winter. Midday is the only time of day when the Sun is in the same direction all year round – due south. This knowledge was used in early times to make the first type of sundial, called the noon-dial. This was a rod sticking out from a south-facing wall. The rod is called a gnomon. It was used to show when to ring the church bells at noon. Very early clocks (13th century) were not very reliable, so the noon-dial was also used to correct public clocks. People would also set their watches by the noon-dial.

A sundial that tells the correct time all day must allow for the tilt of the Earth. One kind of sundial that does this is the equatorial dial.

A noon-dial was used by people to correct their watches and public clocks.

An equatorial dial is a model of the Earth's equator with the polar axis in place (the polar axis is an imaginary line connecting the North and South Poles). The diagram will help you to understand.

The polar axis of the equatorial dial must be parallel to the Earth's own polar axis. For example, London, England, is at a latitude of 51.5°N. A sundial in London must be tilted at 51.5°, as shown in the diagram.

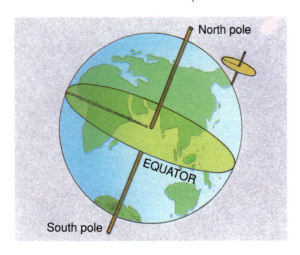

Above A diagram to show a model of an equatorial dial, as compared with the tilt of the Earth.

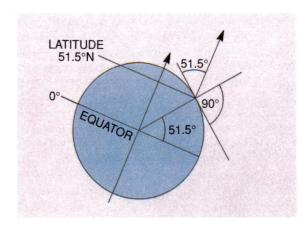

Right A diagram to show the tilt of an equatorial dial at the latitude of London.

ACTIVITY

MAKING A SUMMER EQUATORIAL DIAL

> **YOU NEED**
>
> - a piece of card, 15 cm × 30 cm
> - a protractor
> - a ruler
> - a pencil
> - scissors
> - Sellotape
> - glue
> - a gnomon (20 cm of thin rod or stiff wire)
> - a compass

1 Crease and fold the card in half.
2 Draw a line down the centre on both sides of the card.
3 Measure 10 cm along the centre line from the crease and make a small hole.

The equatorial dial at St Catherine's Dock, near Greenwich. It is tilted to an angle of 51.5°.

4 Repeat step 3, 12.5 cm from the crease on the other half of the card.

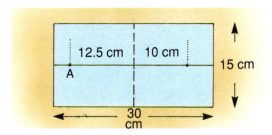

5 Measure 8 cm from the end of the gnomon. Wind some Sellotape around it to form a stop.

6 Use the protractor to mark the hour lines at 15° from the centre line.

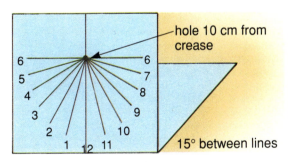

7 Push the gnomon through the dial face. Glue the short end in hole A.
8 Gently hold the dial face down to the sticky tape. Stop and glue it in place.

9 To tell the time, the gnomon must face north. Use the compass to find the direction. Set the dial up in a sunny spot to tell the time.

GARDEN SUNDIALS

On an equatorial dial, every hour is marked as 15°, because the surface on which it is marked is parallel to the Earth's equator. However, you may be more familiar with the horizontal, or garden, sundial. This is the most common type of sundial, and is a horizontal, flat plate with the hour lines marked on it. A triangular gnomon is fixed to the plate to cast the shadow. One advantage of the garden sundial over the equatorial dial is that the garden dial can be used to tell the time all year round. However, the dial will work only if it is pointing due north.

Because of the position of the sundial's plate, the hour divisions are not equal. A different dial has to be made for each latitude, and a special device is made to help construct it.

A garden sundial in a park. This type, also known as a horizontal dial, has an advantage over the equatorial dial – it can be used to tell the time all year round.

ACTIVITY

YOU NEED

- two triangles of stiff card
- an atlas to find your latitude
- a protractor
- a ruler
- a pencil
- a large sheet of paper
- a sheet of plywood
- sticky tape
- a waterproof marker

4 Stand the device on the paper. Mark the hour lines and the back corner on the paper.

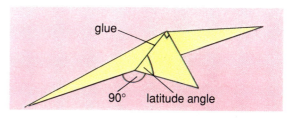

5 Join up the points that you have marked. Add the 6.00 lines and those for 5.00 and 7.00.

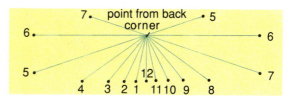

6 Measure the angles. Transfer the information to the sheet of plywood. Mark all the lines in permanent (waterproof) marker.

7 Set up the dial facing north. The best position is a sunny spot that gets no shadow at any time of day.

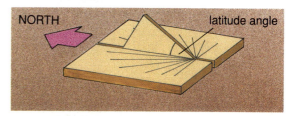

1 Draw and cut out the two cardboard triangles. Make the small one first — you need it to draw the large one.

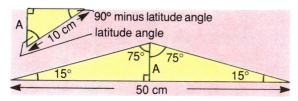

2 Mark out the 15° angles on the larger one.

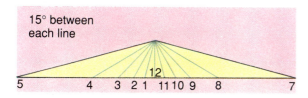

3 Use sticky tape to fix the two triangles together.

TEST YOURSELF

1. What is a noon-dial? How was it first used?
2. What is an equatorial sundial?
3. What advantage has a horizontal, or garden, sundial over an equatorial dial?
4. How does a garden sundial differ from an equatorial sundial?

TIME ZONES

You know that the Earth revolves once in 24 hours. Because there are 360° in a circle, every place on Earth travels through 360° in 24 hours. This means that any point travels through 15° every hour (360° ÷ 24 = 15°).

Imagine slicing the top off the Earth at the latitude of London (51.5°) to reveal a circle. You could mark the angles around the circle, starting with 0° at Greenwich, London. Although there are 360° in a circle, we do not show them as 0° to 360°. Instead, they are shown as 0° to 180° west of Greenwich and 0° to 180° east of Greenwich. If lines are drawn through these points around the globe, from the North Pole to the South Pole, they form lines of longitude.

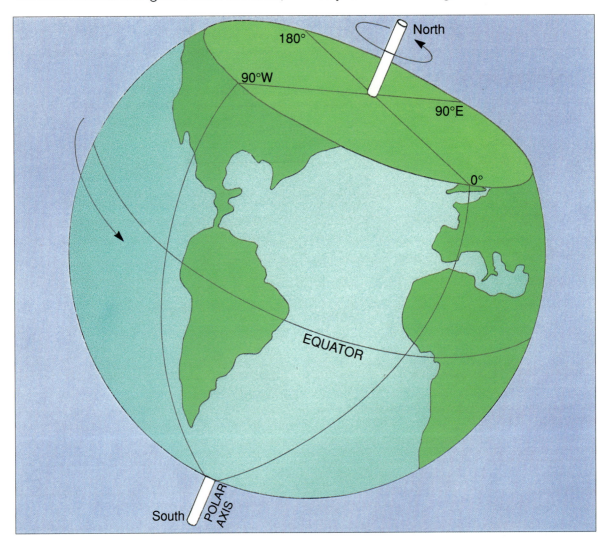

A diagram to show the Earth, sectioned at 51.5° of latitude. The lines of longitude are marked from Greenwich (0°) to 180°E or 180°W.

ACTIVITY

A diagram to show the Earth, seen from above the North Pole on 21 March or 22 September (when the days are exactly 12 hours long).

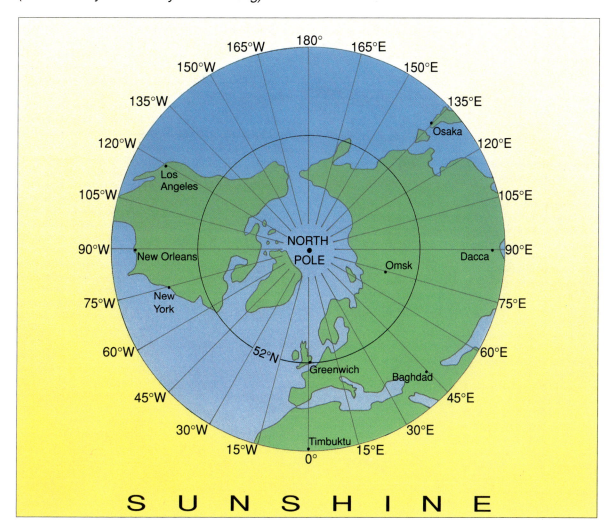

The diagram shows the Earth from over the North Pole. The Sun is at its highest over Greenwich, so it is noon, or 12.00, by the Sun in Greenwich.

The date is one of the two times each year when there are 12 hours of daylight and 12 hours of darkness all over the world.

Each line of longitude shown is at one hour's difference from the next. For example, it is five hours before noon in New York, USA — 7.00 solar time (time by the Sun).

Try to answer the following questions:

What time is it in Timbuktu?
How long is it since the Sun set in Osaka?
Is it sunrise or sunset in New Orleans?
What is the time difference between Omsk and Baghdad?
Is it morning or afternoon in Baghdad?
When the Sun sets in Omsk, how many hours will pass before sunrise in Los Angeles?

You have learned that the Earth rotates through 15° of longitude every hour. If two people live 15° of longitude apart, the person further west will always be one hour in time (according to the Sun) behind the other person. This means that if the person to the east sees that it is 12.00 by his or her sundial, it would be only 11.00 for the person to the west. Every place east or west of another place will have its own local time.

Before 1880, different places in Britain had different local times − even in places quite close to each other. This was not a problem, because most people did not travel far or fast. However, this changed when the railways came. People started to travel rapidly between towns and to cover larger distances. They found it very inconvenient to have to put their watches back as they travelled west, or forward as they travelled east. Also, the train timetable at each station was different. Something had to be done to improve this situation. In 1880, a standard 'time zone' was introduced for Britain and from then on, everywhere had the same time. This made travel much easier.

The world is now divided up into 24 time zones, each one 15° wide. You now have to change your watch by only one hour if you move into the next time zone.

The fastest train in the world − the French TGV. When the railways came, standard time zones had to be introduced to avoid confusion.

When you travel by aircraft, you often have to change your watch by one or more hours, as you move from one time zone to another.

ACTIVITY

YOU NEED

- **a large-scale map of your area, showing degrees of longitude**
- **a watch or clock showing Greenwich Mean Time**

1. Using the map, try to find the longitude of your home to the nearest tenth of a degree.
2. Look at the watch. This is the 'local time' at Greenwich (0° longitude).
3. Each degree is equal to 4 minutes of time (60 minutes ÷ 15°).
4. If you live west of Greenwich, take away this time. If you live east, add on this time.

TEST YOURSELF

1. What are lines of longitude? How are they labelled?
2. Through how many degrees of longitude does the Earth rotate every hour?
3. How many time zones are there in the world?
4. By how much must you change your watch if you travel through two time zones to the east?

23

SUN AND EARTH

You have learnt that the Earth moves around the Sun in a large, almost circular path called an orbit. The distance from the Earth to the Sun is also very large. It is, on average, 150 million km. To show you how far this is, imagine that you could drive from the Earth to the Sun in a fast car. If you kept up a speed of 160 km per hour all the way without stopping, it would take you over 106 years to get there.

The Sun is enormous. It is 109 times larger in diameter than the Earth. A million objects the size of the Earth could be packed inside the Sun and there would still be space left over.

The Sun is not solid like the Earth, but is made up of very hot gases with a surface temperature of 6,000 °C. This is about twice as hot as the hottest coal fire. At the centre of the Sun, the temperature is very much higher: around 15 million °C.

The Sun is made up of very hot gases. The surface reaches 6,000 °C.

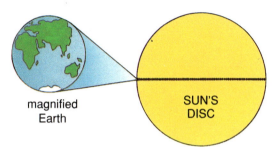

109 Earths, placed side by side, would just cross the Sun's disc.

The Sun does not burn like a coal fire, but produces all its light and heat by changing one kind of gas (hydrogen) into another (helium). This is called a 'nuclear fusion reaction'. This reaction causes the Sun to send out large amounts of light and heat, which travel out into space. Without the Sun's heat and light, we, and all life on Earth, would not be here.

ACTIVITY

Before moving on, it is worth looking at the Sun and Earth as a model, just to be sure you understand their sizes and how far apart they are.

YOU NEED

- **a mustard seed or poppy seed**
- **a grapefruit (about 10 cm in diameter)**
- **11 m of string**
- **a friend**

1. Put the grapefruit in the middle of your playground. The grapefruit is a model of the Sun.
2. Ask your friend to hold one end of the string above the grapefruit.
3. Walk away with the other end of the string until it is tight.

4. Hold the seed next to the end of the string. The seed is a model of the Earth.
5. Walk slowly round the grapefruit, keeping the string tight. You are the Earth orbiting the Sun!

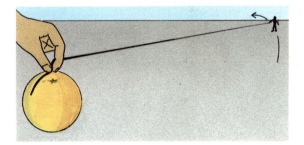

TEST YOURSELF

1. Why is the Sun so important to us?
2. If the Earth was a model 2 cm across, how big would a model of the Sun have to be?
3. How does the Sun produce all its heat and light?

THE MOON — OUR SATELLITE

Just as the Earth travels round the Sun, so the Moon travels round the Earth. It is our satellite. It is much smaller in diameter than Earth — only 3,476 km. The Moon is quite close to us in space. Its average distance from the Earth is 384,000 km. This is 400 times closer than the Sun.

The Moon has no light of its own. It shines because the Sun lights it up, just as the Sun lights up the Earth. Because of this, only half of the Moon's surface will have sunlight on it at any time. As the Moon moves round the Earth, we see different amounts of the sunlit side. This makes it appear to change its shape. These different shapes are called phases. The diagram below shows you how the Moon appears to change as it moves round the Earth.

It takes the Moon 29.5 days to pass through all of its phases. This is known as a 'lunar month'. People who lived thousands of years ago used the Moon's phases as a way of telling time.

Although the Earth and Moon are close together in space and move round the Sun together, they are different in many ways.

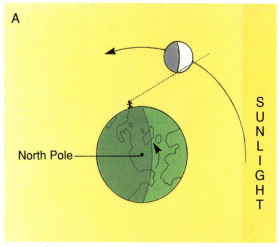
▲ View from space

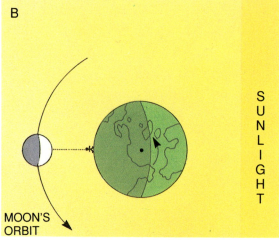
▲ View from space nearly 2 weeks later

Same as A but view from Earth ▼
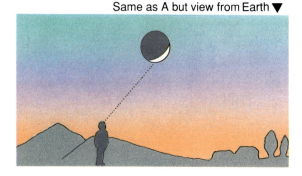

Same as B but view from Earth ▼
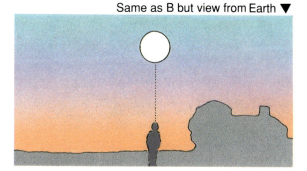

Diagrams to show how the Moon appears from space and from Earth, as it moves around the Earth.

One main difference is their size. This is shown in the picture below.

The Moon has no air or water on its surface. It is a silent world covered with craters and mountains, where no life is to be found.

The Earth and Moon, drawn to scale.

ACTIVITY

YOU NEED

- a light-coloured ball (white is best) on a thread
- a flashlight
- tissue paper (white)
- an elastic band
- 2 friends
- a dark room

1. Cover the front of the flashlight with tissue paper. This will cut down the glare.

2. Stand in the centre of a dark room. You are the Earth.
3. Ask one friend to hold the flashlight about 3 m away and shine it towards you.

4. Ask another friend to move slowly round you, anticlockwise, holding the ball so that you can see it clearly.

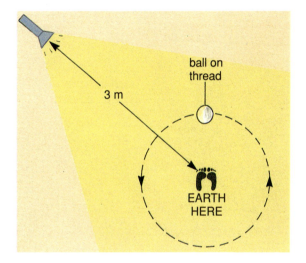

5. Notice how the ball appears to go through 'phases', just as the Moon does.
6. Does your friend holding the flashlight 'see' phases? Try to explain what you have seen.

TEST YOURSELF

1. What is a lunar month? How long is it?
2. As seen from the Moon, would you expect the Earth to show phases? Explain your answer.
3. How does the Moon differ from the Earth?

THE MOON'S SURFACE

On a clear night, especially when the Moon is full, you can see bright and dark patches on its surface. The bright patches are mostly highlands and mountains, and they look bright because they are made of pale rock. The dark patches were once thought to be seas, but are really great, dry plains of dark volcanic rock.

A crater is a shallow hole with a wall around it. The diagram below shows what a crater looks like from the side. Some are very large indeed. The largest crater on the Moon is well over 150 km across.

A side view of a typical lunar crater.

A view of the Moon's surface, taken from space by Apollo 11. *Notice the light and dark areas, and the enormous number of craters.*

A full Moon, as seen from the Earth. This is the best phase of the Moon in which to see the surface markings.

If you use a telescope or powerful binoculars, you will also be able to see the Moon's craters. Most of the craters were made when lumps of rock, called meteors, crashed to the Moon's surface. These meteors came from space. The Moon is covered in craters because there is no atmosphere (air layer). When meteors enter the Earth's atmosphere, most are burnt up due to friction between the meteor and the air. This is one of the reasons why the Earth's surface has very few craters.

The Moon is a strange place. It has no air to scatter sunlight, so the sky is always black, even during the day. If you were to stand on the Moon's surface, you would see the Sun shining out of a black sky. You would also see stars during the day, because there would be no blue sky to blot them out.

The first humans to stand on the Moon's surface were two Americans called Neil Armstrong and Buzz Aldrin. They landed early in the morning of 21 July 1969, having reached the Moon in *Apollo 11.*

ACTIVITY

LOOKING AT THE MOON

YOU NEED

- a clear night when the Moon is visible (you can find this out from a daily newspaper)
- your unaided eyes or binoculars
- a sketch pad
- a pencil
- a flashlight

1. Look carefully at the Moon. Notice the light and dark markings on its surface. The dark markings show up best on a full Moon.
2. Draw the Moon's surface in as much detail as you can.
3. Display your drawings at school and compare them with those of your friends.
4. Try drawing the Moon on different nights when the Moon shows different phases. Do you always see the same markings in the same place on the Moon's surface? Try to explain your answer.

THE FIRST MOON LANDING

YOU NEED

- information from page 28
- the timeline from page 9

1. Mark the first Moon landing on your timeline.
2. Find out all you can about the Moon landings. Plot the dates of them all on your timeline.

One of the astronauts climbing from the lunar module of Apollo 11. *Neil Armstrong and Buzz Aldrin were the first humans on the Moon.*

TEST YOURSELF

1. When the Sun sets on the Earth, the sky stays light for a little while. This is known as twilight. Why does twilight not happen on the Moon?
2. What are the Moon's 'seas'?
3. Why are there very few craters on the Earth, compared with the Moon's surface?

ECLIPSES

From time to time, the Moon passes in front of the Sun and casts a long shadow that touches the Earth's surface. The diagram shows this happening.

Anyone standing in this 'Moon shadow' would see the Sun disappear. This is called a total solar eclipse and it is very exciting to watch. Total solar eclipses last only a few minutes, but during that time the day becomes like night. Birds stop singing, just as they would at night, and stars can be seen in the sky. An eclipse of the Sun can be seen over only a small part of the Earth's surface.

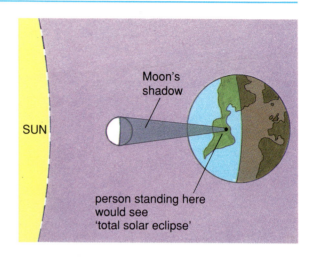

Above A diagram to show the Moon casting a shadow on the Earth during a total eclipse of the Sun.

Left A total eclipse of the Sun, as seen on 7 March 1970. The Moon blocked out the Sun for three-and-a-half minutes.

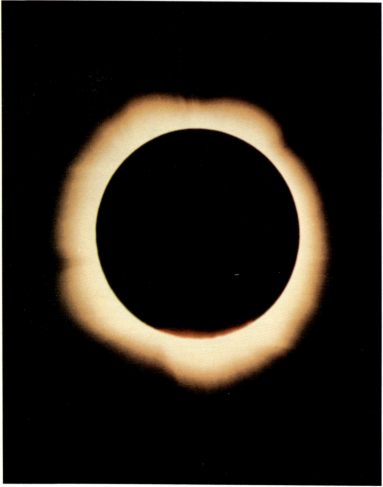

This is because the Moon casts a small, circular shadow on our planet, which covers only a small area. But this small shadow will travel many thousands of kilometres across the Earth's surface before the eclipse is finished.

For an eclipse of the Sun to happen, the Sun, Moon and Earth must all be in a straight line. This does not happen every month, because the Moon's orbit is slightly tilted compared with the straight line joining the Sun and Earth.

When the Moon is far above or below the line joining the Sun and Earth, the Moon's shadow misses the Earth completely, so there is no eclipse. This happens most of the time.

There is another kind of eclipse, called an eclipse of the Moon (lunar eclipse). This occurs when the Moon passes through the Earth's shadow, as shown in the picture below. Even when the Moon is in the Earth's shadow, it is still faintly visible. This is because the air that surrounds the Earth bends some sunlight into the shadow. This gives the Moon a reddish-brown colour.

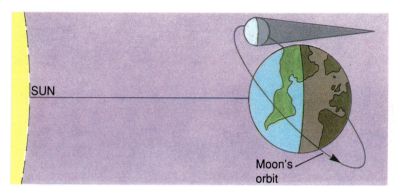

A diagram to show the most common positions of the Sun, Moon and Earth. The Moon is too far above the imaginary straight line between the Sun and the Earth, so there is no eclipse.

A diagram to show an eclipse of the Moon.

TEST YOURSELF

1. How does a total solar eclipse happen?
2. Why are solar eclipses quite uncommon?
3. How does a lunar eclipse happen?
4. Why is the Moon still faintly visible during a lunar eclipse?

THE SOLAR SYSTEM

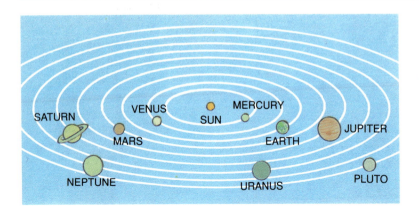

A diagram of the solar system. All the planets move round the Sun in the same direction.

So far, you have found out about the Sun, Moon and Earth. You know that the Moon travels round the Earth once every month, and that the Moon and Earth travel together round the Sun once every year.

But there are other planets travelling around the Sun. These planets, along with other objects called comets and asteroids, make up what we call the solar system. This is the Sun and everything that travels round it.

Five of the planets are bright enough to be seen with the unaided eye. This is why they were discovered by people in ancient times. They are Mercury, Venus, Mars, Jupiter and Saturn. You can spot them quite easily if you know where to look. However, they are not visible all the time. This is because they occasionally move into our daytime sky. Do not expect to find them marked on any star maps, because, unlike the stars, the planets do not remain in any fixed part of the sky.

The William Herschel telescope in La Palma, Mexico. Large telescopes are needed to see Pluto, as it is so far from the Earth. They can also give astronomers much information about the other planets.

However, astronomy magazines publish planetary positions monthly, so you could use one of these to spot your first planet. Venus is very easy to find, because it appears as a brilliant object in the evening sky after sunset for a few weeks, roughly every eighteen months.

The other three members of the solar system are too dim to be seen with the unaided eye, because they are so far away from Earth. They are Uranus, Neptune and Pluto. Uranus and Neptune can be glimpsed with binoculars, but Pluto is so faint that you will need quite a large telescope to see it.

ACTIVITY

A MODEL OF THE SOLAR SYSTEM

YOU NEED

- nine friends
- a playground or field
- a tape measure

1. One person will be the Sun and the rest will be planets.
2. The person who represents the Sun stands in the middle of the playground or field.
3. Each person chooses a planet. Using the list below, work out how far he or she must stand from the Sun. (Let 2 cm equal 1 million km.)

Distance from sun (millions of km)			
Mercury	58	Jupiter	778
Venus	108	Saturn	1427
Earth	150	Uranus	2870
Mars	228	Neptune	4497
		Pluto	5900

4. Each person uses the tape to measure his or her distance from the Sun. Check your answers with your friends to make sure that all the distances are correct.
5. Take up your positions.

6. What do you notice about the distances of the four planets closest to the Sun?
7. Are the orbits in the solar system evenly spread out?
8. Which planet would you expect to take the longest time to travel round the Sun? Which would you expect to take the shortest time?

TEST YOURSELF

1. Why can you not always see the bright planets?
2. Why are the planets not marked on star maps?
3. Which planets cannot be seen with the unaided eye?

THE PLANETS

You have seen how the planets move around the Sun. The ancient Greeks noticed the movements of five of them against the background of stars and called them 'planets', which means wanderers. We now know of eight other planets in the solar system besides the Earth. Here is a brief look at each one.

Mercury, the closest planet to the Sun, is a little larger than our Moon. Like the Moon, Mercury has no atmosphere and is covered in craters. It has no satellites (moons).

Venus, next to Mercury, is almost the same size as the Earth, and has been called the Earth's twin. However, Venus is very different. The whole planet is completely covered in cloud, and its atmosphere contains a vast amount of carbon dioxide gas. This has caused a very strong greenhouse effect, making Venus's surface too hot for life to exist. Venus is thought by many scientists to be a lesson for us on Earth: an example of what might happen if we continue to release large amounts of carbon dioxide into our atmosphere.

Mars, the famous Red Planet, lies beyond the Earth's orbit. Mars is just over half the size of the Earth, and has two satellites. It was once thought that life might exist on Mars and in 1976 two space probes went there to look, but no life was found.

Jupiter is the giant of the solar system. It is covered in clouds, and is striped, but its best known feature is the Great Red Spot, which is thought to be a huge, permanent storm. Jupiter has sixteen satellites, some of which can be seen through strong binoculars.

Saturn, the famous ringed planet, is a beautiful sight through a telescope. It is only slightly smaller than Jupiter, but twice as far away from Earth. It has seventeen satellites.

Uranus is smaller than both Jupiter and Saturn and is the first of the planets to be discovered using a telescope. It was discovered in 1781 by the amateur astronomer William Herschel, using a homemade telescope from his back garden. It has fifteen satellites. In 1977, it was discovered to have rings.

Neptune was discovered by 1846, but not by accident. Astronomers began looking for it when they discovered something was 'pulling' Uranus out of position. Two men, Adams and Leverrier, worked out where to look, and the planet was found by two German astronomers – Galle and D'Arrest.

Pluto, thought to be the outermost planet, is a mystery. It is as small as our Moon, and may not deserve the title of planet, as it seems to be nothing like any of the other

A diagram to show the planets of the solar system to scale.

planets. It was found in 1930 by the astronomer Clyde Tombaugh, who discovered it on photographs taken through a large telescope. In 1978, it was found to have a satellite. With the discovery of Pluto, the size of the solar system was increased by over four times that known to the ancient astronomers.

ACTIVITIES

> **YOU NEED**
> - **the timeline from chapter 2**

Plot the discoveries of Uranus, Neptune and Pluto on your timeline.

FINDING OUT ABOUT THE SOLAR SYSTEM

Astronomers have found out a lot about the other planets in the solar system. Many of the new discoveries have come from space probes, such as *Voyager I* and *II*. You can find out about these for yourself from the many new astronomy books and magazines that are available.

You can also find out about other objects in the solar system, such as asteroids and comets.

> **YOU NEED**
> - **a library with up-to-date books on the planets and solar system**

1. Work as a group. Each person should choose a planet (or more than one, if you are in a small group).
2. Find out as much as you can about your chosen planet.
3. Find out about the other objects in our solar system, such as asteroids and comets.
4. Make a group display at school, showing your findings.

This photograph of Saturn was taken by one of the Voyager space probes. These spacecraft have given astronomers a great deal of information about our solar system.

TEST YOURSELF

1. What does the word 'planet' mean?
2. Which planets were known before telescopes were invented?
3. Name the largest planet in the solar system.

THE SUN — OUR STAR

You have learnt that the Sun is a large ball of hot gas that sends us all our heat and light. It is so bright that it is very dangerous to look at it directly. Astronomers often examine the Sun by projecting its image on to a screen. Viewed in this way, the Sun is seen to have dark spots on its surface — they are called sunspots. They are caused by strong magnetic fields on the Sun's surface.

When you stand outside on a clear, dark night and look out at the stars, you are looking at other 'suns' far away in space. Our Sun appears so large and bright only because it is so much nearer to us. Some stars are really much bigger and brighter than the Sun, and appear dim only because they are so much further away. Our star is, of course, very important to us, but is quite small and ordinary when compared with some other stars.

A diagram to show our Sun and some other stars to scale, with their surface temperatures.

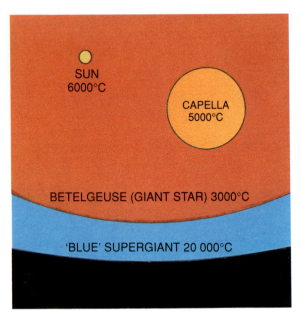

The distances between the stars are very great indeed. If you made a scale model of the solar system with the Sun the size of a table-tennis ball, then Pluto, the furthest planet, would be a speck of dust 150 m away. The nearest star (Proxima Centauri) would be another ball 1000 km away! It can be seen from this that the solar system is very small compared with the distances between the stars. Some astronomers think that there might be planets orbiting other stars. If this is so, then life might exist on some of these planets. Imagine an alien being on some distant planet looking up at the night sky. For that alien, our Sun would be just another small star shining dimly in the night.

A sunspot, photographed by the space shuttle in summer 1985. Sunspots are much cooler than the normal surface temperature of the Sun.

ACTIVITY

LOOKING FOR SUNSPOTS

YOU NEED

- **an adult to help you**
- **binoculars with a stand or tripod**
- **two pieces of white card (about A4 size)**
- **a sharp knife**
- **a ruler**
- **a pencil**
- **sticky tape**

WARNING: never look directly at the Sun with or without binoculars. It is very dangerous and could make you permanently blind.

1. First draw the outline of the binocular lenses on one of the pieces of white card.
2. Ask an adult to cut out the outlines. Do not attempt to do this yourself.

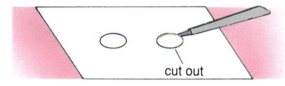
cut out

3. Fix this card to the binoculars with sticky tape.

sticky tape

4. Fix the binoculars on a stand (a tripod is best).
5. Ask an adult to point the binoculars at the Sun.
6. Place the second card in the shadow of the first card (about 30 cm behind). 'Project' the Sun's image on to it.

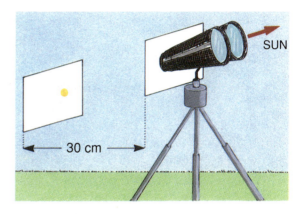
SUN
30 cm

7. Adjust the focus of the binoculars so the Sun's image appears sharp on the card.
8. Look carefully at this image. Can you see any dark markings on the Sun's image? If you can, mark their position on the card.
9. Follow the sunspots every day. You will see that they gradually move across the surface. This is because the Sun, like the Earth, is rotating on its axis.

TEST YOURSELF

1. What is the difference between a star (sun) and a planet?
2. Why do sunspots move?
3. Why do astronomers often project the image of the Sun on to a screen?

THE GALAXY — OUR STAR CITY

If you stand outside on a dark summer's evening, well away from artificial light, and look towards the south, you will see a faint, cloudlike band of light stretching up from the horizon. This faint band of light is called the Milky Way.

Part of the Milky Way — our galaxy — as seen from Earth. The white line is the trail caused by a satellite.

If you look carefully, you will see that the Milky Way stretches right across the sky. What you are seeing is the inside of our galaxy. The faint band of light is caused by the glow of millions of distant stars, all lying along a narrow region of sky. The picture below may help you to understand this.

Our galaxy is like a great 'star city' floating in space. The solar system lies a long way from the centre, out in the 'suburbs' of this city. It is very hard to imagine the size of our galaxy. Astronomers have measured its size, but they do not use kilometres; instead, they measure these enormous distances in light years. A light year is the distance a ray of light will travel in one year. Light travels very fast indeed; if you switch on a torch, the beam will move away from you at 300,000 km every second. At this speed, it would take just over a second to reach the Moon, and only eight-and-a-half minutes to reach the Sun. But, even at this speed, it would take the beam of light 100,000 years to travel across our galaxy.

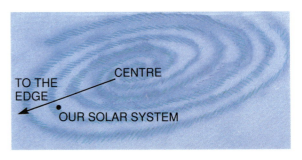

A diagram to show how our galaxy would appear from the outside.

Astronomers using large telescopes have discovered millions of other galaxies far beyond our own. The nearest one is called the Andromeda Galaxy. It is the furthest object we can see with the unaided eye. It is worth trying to catch a glimpse of this faint object, for the light you see has had to travel for 2 million years to reach you.

The Andromeda Galaxy is the nearest galaxy to our own. It is the furthest object that we can see with the unaided eye.

ACTIVITIES

FINDING THE MILKY WAY

> **YOU NEED**
> - a clear, dark night (August or February are the best months)
> - a place well away from street lights
> - no moonlight
> - binoculars
> - a clear view to the south
> - a star map

1. Look towards the south around 9.00-9.30 p.m.
2. Allow at least 10 minutes for your eyes to adjust to the dark.
3. Try to pick out the faint band of light stretching up from the horizon. It will look like a long, ragged cloud.
4. Follow it with your eyes, up over your head and down towards the northern horizon.
5. Try to explore it with binoculars. You will see many faint stars and glimpse clouds of hydrogen gas.
6. Use a star map to find your way around the Milky Way. Check what you have seen from the star maps and learn more about them.

FINDING THE ANDROMEDA GALAXY

> **YOU NEED**
> - an evening in autumn
> - a dark, clear, moonless night
> - a place well away from street lights
> - a star map

1. Find the 'Square of Pegasus' on your star map. Find it in the sky.
2. Look at the drawing below. this shows you where to look for the Andromeda Galaxy.

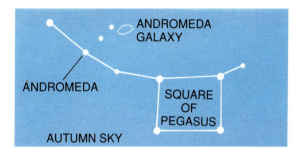

3. Allow 10 minutes for your eyes to adjust to the dark. The Andromeda Galaxy will appear as a faint fuzzy blob.
4. Try looking just to the side of it – that will make it easier to see. Think about how long the light has had to travel before it reaches your eyes.

TEST YOURSELF

1. Is the solar system closer to the centre or the edge of our galaxy?
2. What is the Milky Way?
3. If you could travel at the speed of light, how long would it take you:
    - to travel to the Sun?
    - to travel right across our galaxy?

CONSTELLATIONS

A diagram to show some of the main constellations that appear at different times of year.

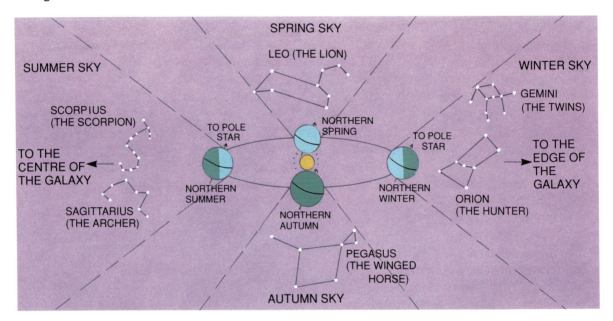

A constellation is the name astronomers give to a group of stars that seems to form a pattern. Many of the constellations we see today were named by people thousands of years ago. The ancient astronomers thought that some star patterns resembled heroes and creatures from their legends. Only a few constellations really look like the things they are supposed to represent. It seems that ancient astronomers had very good imaginations!

The constellations are useful signposts for finding our way about the sky. As the Earth travels round the Sun, we see different constellations at different times of year.

In summer, the night side of the Earth is turned towards the centre of our galaxy. When we look in that direction, we see constellations such as Scorpius and Sagittarius. In winter, our night sky faces the other way. Therefore, we see the constellations lying in that direction, such as Orion and Gemini.

Most of the stars belonging to a constellation lie at different distances from us and each other, so constellations do not really exist in space. They are just the patterns formed by stars lying in the same direction, as seen from the Earth.

All the stars we can see with the unaided eye belong to our galaxy. The closest star to the solar system is Proxima Centauri, which is 4.3 light years away. This means that light takes 4.3 years to reach us from Proxima Centauri.

You have learnt that our galaxy is only one among millions of other galaxies. These galaxies make up what we call the Visible Universe. The Universe is everything that exists. Astronomers have discovered that the galaxies are moving away from each other, so that the Universe is gradually spreading out, or expanding.

ACTIVITY

MAKE A CONSTELLATION

> WARNING: ask an adult to help you stick the wires into the polystyrene balls.

YOU NEED

- 5 or more polystyrene balls
- 5 or more differing lengths of stiff wire
- Plasticine
- a dark-coloured piece of card (about A2 size)
- a table or worktop

1. Stick the end of each piece of wire into each polystyrene ball, with the help of an adult.
2. Stick the other end of each wire into some Plasticine to act as a base.
3. Set up the balls on the table or worktop. Arrange them so that they are not all in a line.
4. Place the dark card behind the balls, so that they are easier to see.
5. Move about 2 m to 3 m from the nearest ball, and view the pattern of balls with one eye. Draw what you see.

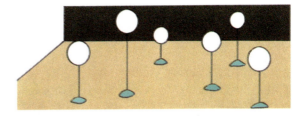

6. Move the balls into different positions on the table and repeat the activity.
7. Do all the balls appear to be at the same distance from you? What does this tell you about constellations?

LOOKING AT SOME CONSTELLATIONS

YOU NEED

- a map of the night sky
- a dark, clear, moonless night
- a dim flashlight

1. Look at your star map and find the Pole Star.
2. Find the constellations Cassiopeia and Ursa Major. They are close to the Pole Star. Both are easy to spot and are above the horizon all year round for people living above latitude 50°N. Cassiopeia looks like a W or M and Ursa Major looks like a saucepan.
3. Draw these star patterns. Notice how they move round the sky during the year.

TEST YOURSELF

1. What is a constellation?
2. Why do constellations not really exist in space?
3. Why do we see different constellations at different times of year?

NAVIGATION BY THE SUN

Sailors often travel for days without spotting any landmarks, so it is important for them to have some means of finding their position. If sailors can work out their latitude and longitude, then they know exactly where they are on Earth.

LATITUDE

You know from your work on the seasons that the Sun rises higher in the sky in the summer and lower in the winter. It is fairly simple to calculate the angle of the noon Sun above the horizon for every latitude from one known angle at any place. The diagram shows how this can be done. This can be repeated for every day of the year. Books of tables of the Sun's angle at local noon for all latitudes and dates are available.

'Shooting the Sun' is the sailor's term for measuring the angle between the horizon and the Sun. It is done with a device called a sextant. It is very dangerous to look directly at the Sun with the unaided eye, so a sextant has dark filters to make it safer. But incorrect use can still be dangerous. A sextant uses two mirrors to bring images of the Sun and the horizon into line in a small telescope. When they line up, the angle between them can be read from a scale. Then the latitude can be looked up in the tables.

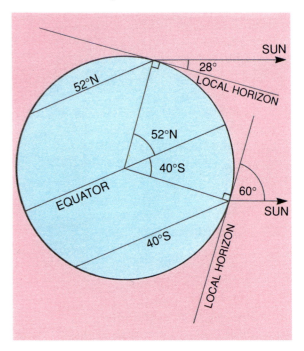

Above A diagram to show how the angle of the noon Sun can be calculated at latitude 52°N. On this day, the Sun is 28° above the horizon. The drawing shows how this angle can be found at any latitude.

A diagram to show a sextant. This is often called an 'instrument of double reflection', because it has two mirrors.

LONGITUDE

You know that the Earth rotates through 15° every hour. This means that a particular time of day (for example, midday) 'moves' around the Earth. Because of the direction of the Earth's spin, every hour westward of a given place is 15° of longitude (see page 20). Early navigators also knew this, but they could not make use of the information because they had no accurate way of keeping time.

To find your longitude, it is necessary to have a good means of telling time. You need to use a sextant to tell when it is noon by the Sun wherever you are on Earth. You also need to know what time it is at Greenwich, which is 0° longitude. Using these two times, find the difference in hours between your location and Greenwich. Then multiply this time by 15°. This gives your longitude in degrees. Page 20 will help you to see why this is so.

In 1760, John Harrison made the idea practical by inventing the first portable, reliable and accurate ship's clock, called a chronometer. With such a clock, a ship's navigator always knows the time at Greenwich. This means that the crew can always find its longitude, wherever it is in the world.

By the end of the eighteenth century, sailors could plot their longitudinal position using John Harrison's invention, the chronometer.

TEST YOURSELF

1. What is 'shooting the Sun'?
2. How does a sextant work?
3. Why was the invention of the chronometer so important?

SPACESHIP EARTH

You have found out that the Earth is just one of nine planets moving around the Sun, and that our Sun is just one star among millions of other stars in orbit around our galaxy. You also know that our galaxy is just one among millions of other galaxies that make up the Universe. Seen from this point of view, our planet seems very unimportant — just a tiny planet moving through the vastness of space.

However, our planet is very important to us — we depend on it completely. It has been said that the Earth is like a spaceship; that is a very good description. Every spaceship's crew must have clean air to breathe, protection from dangerous radiation (such as ultraviolet rays), supplies of food and water, a temperature control system and a good waste-recycling system. Like any spaceship, the Earth has to supply all the needs of its crew. If we (the crew) are to survive, we must take good care of our ship's 'life-support' systems.

Of course, our planet's life-support systems are far more complicated than those of a spaceship, because the Earth contains so many different forms of life, all living together and depending on each other. But the principle is the same.

You have probably read or heard that some of these systems are being harmed: the ozone layer in the Earth's atmosphere, which protects us from ultraviolet rays; the tropical rainforests that help to regulate world weather patterns; the rivers, seas and lakes and the air that we breathe. Resources, such as coal, oil and metals, are being used up at alarming rates and cannot be replaced.

These life-support systems have existed for millions of years, and the damage is being done by one section of the 'crew' — humans. However, more and more people are becoming aware of the dangers created by human activity. For example, many countries have banned the use of CFCs (chlorofluorocarbons) — chemicals that damage the ozone layer. Much effort is being made to reduce the amount of air pollutiion, from power stations, factories and cars.

Smog looms over the San Bernadino Mountains in California, USA. This is air pollution belched out by power stations, factories and cars.

It is important to protect our environment. One step that can be taken is to recycle waste, which usually contains precious resources. Here, household rubbish is being recycled at a special plant.

Governments and other groups are campaigning to get people to save energy, reduce and recycle waste and use household chemicals that do not damage the environment.

These are just a few examples of how humans can save our planet's life-support systems from further destruction. Everyone can help in some way to keep our 'spaceship' in good working order. After all, we really have no choice — at the moment, there is nowhere else to go.

ACTIVITY

1 Find out about any schemes in your area that have been set up to help preserve the environment. Some examples are waste recycling, anti-litter campaigns and saving energy.
2 Find out all you can about the harm that is being done to our environment. See if you can discover what is being done, or suggested, to stop the damage. Page 44 will give you some ideas of areas to study.

Litter is not only ugly — it can cause serious damage to wildlife and the environment. However, it is easy to avoid dropping litter.

TEST YOURSELF

1. Why is the description 'Spaceship Earth' such a good one?
2. Name three of the Earth's life-support systems that are being harmed by human activity.

Glossary

Alien A person or creature from another world.
Asteroids Thousands of small, rock-like objects orbiting the Sun between Mars and Jupiter. They range from 670 km in diameter to less than 1 km.
Astronomer A scientist who studies objects in space and the whole Universe.
Comet A ball of ice, gas and dust, moving in the solar system. Comets are sometimes seen to form long tails.
Crater A hole in the surface of a planet or moon, usually made by a meteorite.
Equator An imaginary circle running round the centre of the Earth. It divides the Earth into the northern and southern hemispheres. Any line of longitude is at right angles to the equator. Any line of latitude is parallel.
Friction The force created by two objects or materials when rubbed together. The rubbing creates heat.
Galaxy A very large collection of stars moving together in space.
Greenhouse effect This is caused when certain gases (e.g. carbon dioxide) slow down the loss of heat from the Earth into space, causing the atmosphere to heat up.
Greenwich Mean Time The local time at the 0° line of longitude passing through Greenwich, England — a standard time for Britain and from which times throughout most of the world are calculated.
Horizon A distant point where the sky appears to meet the land.
Latitude The imaginary lines that run east to west right around the Earth. They are parallel to the equator.
Longitude The imaginary lines that run north to south right around the Earth. They are at right angles to the equator.
Lunar To do with the Moon.
Meteor A piece of rock that travels through space until it falls within the gravitational field of a star or planet.
Navigator The person on a ship (or any other form of transport) who works out the position and course to follow.
Nuclear fusion reaction The process of fusing atoms together to form new types of atom. During this process, large amounts of heat and light are released.
Orbit A curved path followed by one object (in space) around another, larger object.
Panorama The view all the way around the horizon.
Satellite An object in space that is in orbit around a larger body.
Solar To do with the Sun.
Ultraviolet rays The rays from the Sun that burn and brown the skin. They can cause serious harm to living things.
Unaided eye Your eyesight without the use of a telescope, binoculars or other optical instrument.

Books to read

Astronomy for Starters Robin Scagell (George Philip, 1987)
Astronomy for the Under Tens Patrick Moore (George Philip, 1987)
Our Future in Space Tim Furniss (Wayland, 1985)

Pocket Book of Astronomy James Muirden (Kingfisher, 1990)
The Solar System Robin Kerrod (Wayland, 1990)
Stars and Galaxies Robin Kerrod (Wayland, 1990)

Picture acknowledgements

The author and publishers would like to thank the following for allowing illustrations to be reproduced in this book: Roger Browne *frontispiece,*17; Mary Evans Picture Library 8; National Maritime Museum 16; PHOTRI *cover* (top right); TRH 22, 29, 30, 32, 35, 36; Wayland Picture Library 43; ZEFA *cover* (left), 6, 11, 18, 23, 24, 28 (right), 38, 44, 45. All inside artwork is by Jenny Hughes. Cover artwork is by Marilyn Clay.

Index

Air 6, 7, 27, 28, 44
Aldrin, Buzz 28
Andromeda Galaxy 38, 39
Apollo 11 28
Aristotle 8, 9
Armstrong, Neil 28
Asteroids 32
Astronomers 8, 34, 35, 36, 38, 40
Astronomy 9, 33
Atmosphere 34
Australia 10
Autumn 10

Binoculars 28, 29, 34

Carbon dioxide 34
CFCs 44
Chronometer 43
Comets 32
Constellations 40-41
Copernicus 8, 9
Craters 27, 28, 29, 34

Equator 12, 14, 18
Equatorial dial 16, 17, 18

Galaxy 38-39, 40, 44
Galileo 9
Garden sundials 18
Gnomon 16, 17, 18
Great Red Spot 34
Greenhouse effect 34
Greenwich 20, 21, 23, 43
    Mean Time 15, 23

Harrison, John 43
Heat 24, 25, 36
Herschel, William 34
Horizontal sundial 18

Jupiter 32, 34

Latitude 12, 13, 14, 16, 18, 19, 20, 42
Light 10, 24, 25, 36
Light years 38, 40
Longitude 20, 21, 22, 23, 42, 43
Lunar eclipse 31
Lunar month 26, 27

Mars 32, 34
Mercury 32, 34
Meteors 28
Milky Way 38-39
Moon 8, 9, 26, 27, 28, 29, 30, 31, 32, 34, 35, 38

Neptune 33, 34
Noon-dial 16
North Pole 6, 10, 13, 16, 20
Nuclear fusion reaction 24

Orbit 6, 14, 24, 31, 34, 44
Ozone layer 44

Phases of the Moon 26, 27
Planets 8, 9, 32-33, 34-35, 44
Pluto 33, 35, 36
Polar axis 16
Pollution 44
Proxima Centauri 36, 40
Ptolemy 9

Rainforests 44

Saturn 32
Seasons 12
Sextant 42
Solar eclipse 30-31
Solar system 32, 33, 34, 35, 36, 38
South Pole 10, 13, 16, 20

Space probes 34
Spin of the Earth 6, 7, 8, 10, 20, 22, 43,
Spring 10
Stars 8, 30, 32, 36, 38, 40, 42, 44
Summer 10, 14, 15, 28, 40
Sun 6, 7, 8, 9, 10, 12, 14, 15, 16, 21, 24, 25, 26, 28, 30, 31, 32, 33, 34, 36-37, 38, 42, 43, 44
Sundials 16-19, 22
Sunlight 6, 26, 28
Sunspots 36, 37

Telescope 28, 33, 34, 35
Time zones 22, 23
Tombaugh, Clyde 35

Ultraviolet rays 44
Universe 40, 41
Uranus 33, 34
USA 21, 28, 44

Venus 32, 33, 34

Water 6, 7, 27, 44
Winter 10, 14, 16, 42